INSTAGRAM YOUR WAY TO SUCCESS

INCREASE YOUR SALES, MARKET YOUR PRODUCTS AND LAUNCH YOUR BRAND WITH SOCIAL MEDIA

BY SMART READS

Free Audiobook

As a thank you for being a Smart Reader you can choose 2 FREE audiobooks from audible.com. Simply sign up for free by visiting www.audibletrial.com/Travis to get your books.

Visit:
www.smartreads.co/freebooks
to receive Smart Reads books for FREE

Check us out on Instagram:
www.instagram.com/smart_readers
@smart_readers

ABOUT SMARTREADS

Choose Smart Reads and get smart every time. Smart Reads sorts through all the best content and condenses the most helpful information into easily digestible chunks.

We design our books to be short, easy to read and highly informative. Leaving you with maximum understanding in the least amount of time.

Smart Reads aims to accelerate the spread of quality information so we've taken the copyright off everything we publish and donate our material directly to the public domain. You can read our uncopyright below.

We believe in paying it forward and donate 5% of our net sales to Pencils of Promise to build schools, train teachers and support child education.

To limit our footprint and restore forests around the globe we are planting a tree for every 10 hardcover books we sell.

Thanks for choosing Smart Reads and helping us help the planet.

Sincerely,

Travis & the Smart Reads Team

TABLE OF CONTENTS

INTRODUCTION

Twitter is basically dying. Facebook is still awesome, and of course you need a Facebook profile to help build your brand. But Instagram is where the people who love visuals can be found. And in 2017, more and more of people are preferring visuals more than anything.

Most people are bored of text. They want to see stuff. They're already looking at your competitors and now they want to see YOU. To make sure you don't fall behind your rivals, it's time to get yourself on Instagram.

But how do you grow your brand here? How do you go from one follower (your spouse) to thousands of followers?

This book will guide you on the process of creating a solid, engaging and even profitable Instagram account to help your brand. You'll learn how to set up an account, build your following, take better photos, and market yourself so that Instagram becomes a place where your brand starts to sell itself.

CHAPTER 1: WHY INSTAGRAM IS THE RIGHT PLACE FOR YOU

Is Instagram for you? Does it have what you need? Is it the right social media platform that's going to help you grow your brand?

Some businesses have been slow to catch on to Instagram, wrongly assuming all this time that Instagram is just for photographers, or cute people who want to take lots of selfies. But Instagram is great for any niche, whether you sell surfboards or writing services.

Let's take a look at a few of its pros:

People Get To See What You're Selling
Some businesses are bad at explaining to their audiences what it is they're selling. They're just not good with words. If you can't explain your product or service in a few words, you'll have a tricky time making any sales. So why don't you take pictures of your product or service instead?

Pictures are a lot easier to understand than words. If you take the right photos, your customers can easily see what it is you sell.

You Could Go Viral

Is a boring product description on your website ever going to go viral? It's unlikely! But images on Instagram always have the potential to go viral.

Imagine if you posted an awesome image of your product, along with eye-catching copy that spoke to your target audience? It's got the potential to be shared across this social media platform, and be seen by thousands of people. That kind of exposure is awesome.

Your Competitors Might Not Be On Instagram Yet

If you're in a niche market, there's a good chance your competitors aren't on Instagram yet.

And it's true - a lot of people have been slow to wake up to the potential of Instagram. Most entrepreneurs assumed it wasn't a good marketplace for their niche.

So get in there and be the first in your niche. Do this and you can gobble up the lion's share of the market before anyone else. You'll have the expertise. You'll be the person everyone has been waiting for all this time.

Instagram is Rapidly Growing

Despite the fact there could be an empty hole in your niche, Instagram is growing at a rapid rate. It's still way behind Facebook in terms of total users, but in terms of engagement (which is more important) it's ahead.

Why? Because people love photos. It only takes us a second or so to be struck by an eye-catching photo. Text, on the other hand, is more time consuming.

Because Instagram is growing its user base all the time, it means more and more people are thirsting for content. So give the people what they want!

It's So Easy To Connect With People
Did you think connecting with people on Instagram was always going to be the hardest bit?

"There are like 300 million users on Instagram. How am I going to make a connection with them? They'll never notice me!"

Actually, it's a lot easier to connect with people on Instagram than it is on Facebook. And this is all down to the power of the hash tag.

Hash tags make it so easier to find the content you're looking for. If someone uses the hash tag "fun" and you type it in, you can find that persons pictures. Hash tags don't cost any money. They're basically free advertising.

You Get To See What Works And What Doesn't
The hardest thing about being in business is you sometimes don't know what people want from you. You come up with what you think is a great product; take it to market ... and then it bombs. Nobody wants it. This is dispiriting, but Instagram can prevent it from happening.

If you've got something new to offer, you can post about it on Instagram and see what happens in real time. You can see whether people are drawn to your product or service, or whether they're repelled by it. This is a great advantage when using Instagram. It will help you avoid taking a product nobody wants, all the way to market.

But What About The Cons?
There are a couple of cons to using Instagram that needs to be highlighted. These don't necessarily need to put you off using Instagram, but they might mean that you need to tweak your methods.

Your Audience Might Not Be On Here
If you have a very niche product, there is a chance your target audience isn't even on Instagram.

You Have To Focus On Organic Traffic
Especially now that Instagram is clamping down on Follow bots, organic traffic might be what you need to rely on. This is time consuming, and will require effort. It's covered in a later chapter of this book.

You Can't Upload Images From Desktop
This is a source of frustration for some. Instagram still won't let users upload from their desktop.

CHAPTER 2: GETTING STARTED

Okay, first the boring bit: Getting started.

If you've opened an Instagram account before, you might be tempted to skip this chapter. Don't. There are also filters, which you might not have heard of, and which will prove handy for you later on.

Instagram is a mobile platform only. You can log in into your account from your desktop, but you can't upload or comment on pictures.

So, the first thing you need to do is download the Instagram app to your Smartphone. Then, register your personal account, and choose a name and password. Then, you'll need to upload a suitable photo for your profile pic and enter up to 150 words in your bio. You don't have to include a bio, but it's essential. However, you can leave it blank for now. You can return to it later.

Once you've set your profile, it will initially be on public display, which means that everyone can see it. If you'd prefer to go private for now, go ahead and swap it. Doing so means that anyone who wants to follow you has to request approval.

Notifications

You'll want to decide how you get your notifications. Head to your settings and open the notification center. You can choose whether you want to receive notifications when you're on the app, or externally (basically, you'll still get notified if someone has liked your photo even if you aren't on the app).

Social Connectivity

Instagram can be used in isolation. But to get the best out of it, it's strongly suggested you use it in tandem with other social media platforms. To this end, you can connect it to the likes of Facebook and Twitter, as well as Flickr and VK. To enhance connectivity, go to the Settings menu and link the profiles.

When you link profiles, your Instagram posts will automatically be visible elsewhere. For example, if you've linked your Instagram account with your Facebook account, all the photos you subsequently upload to Instagram will also be seen on your Facebook wall.

How To Add Photos And Videos

The whole point of Instagram is - as you know - to upload photos and videos. But how do you do that?

You can take a picture or video using the camera button that you'll find at the center of your panel. Or, you can upload a photo or video you've already taken on your phone. Previously, this option was a bit tricky because Instagram made us crop our photos so that they fitted a specific ratio. Fortunately, there are no longer any restrictions.

Editing
If you've ever seen someone upload a photo to Instagram, you'll have noticed that some of the photos appear to have been strongly edited. Instagram indeed has lots of filters that allow you to get creative with your images so you can alter the way they look.

There are some ready-made filters available that you can click and use. Alternatively, you can edit the photos yourself. For example, you can decrease or increase the contrast and brightness, and you can even change the depth of field.

The lux effect is pretty good since it's like an auto-enhancing feature that enriches your photos.

Filters
Even if you've never used Instagram before, you likely know about filters. No doubt you've seen friends

upload pictures with filters. Filters are there to alter the look of your photo, giving it a bit more life.

Here is a quick and brief rundown of some of the most popular filters on Instagram:

- **Normal** - Want to keep the photo like it is? Then choose Normal

- **Lo-Fi** - Lo-fi makes your images warmer and brings out the saturation and shadows

- **EarlyBird** - If you want to make your photo look old, choose this filter

- **Amaro** - This filter blurs out the sides of the picture, shifting focus to the center. It also makes it brighter

- **Rise** - This filter softens the lighting

- **InkWell** - This filter turns your photo black and white. It's nice if you want to create a more mysterious look to your photos

- **Sutro** - This filter creates a burnt effect on the edges of your picture. It also increases the highlights

- **Mayfair** - Want a pinkish tone? This filter does that for you. It also adds a black border.

- **Sierra** - This filter makes your image look faded and softens it up.

- **Valencia** - If you're looking for an antique effect, the Valencia filter can help to this end. It makes your pictures warmer, too

- **Nashville** - As the name might suggest, the Nashville filter creates a look of wistful nostalgia in your pictures. It achieves this with a pink tint while lowering the contrast

- **Toaster** - As its name suggests, the toaster filter "burns" the center of your picture, making it look old. It's quite cool if you want to take a period photo!

- **Perpetua** - Besides having a cool name, the Perpetua filter adds a pastel look to your portraits

- **X-Pro** - Want a tint of gold in your pictures? This is the filter to go for.

- **Cream** - It does what its name suggests, and adds a creamy texture to your images

- **Walden** - Walden boosts exposure levels and adds a yellow tint to photos

- **Aden** - Aden brings out the greens and blues in your pictures

- **Slumber** - Slumber lowers saturation, and brings out the blues and blacks. People like it because it gives their images a slick, retro look.

CHAPTER 3: FOCUS ON INFLUENCE AND NOT FOLLOWERS

Before telling you how to build your Instagram following, it's important to understand that numbers don't matter as much as influence. Knowing this will put you on the right track from the start.

Way too many brands and individuals head into Instagram on a mission to bag as many followers as possible. They think it's absolutely important that they have a million followers. But what you need to do is shift focus from the number of followers you have, to the number of proper, in-depth interactions you make.

A connection with your followers is far more important than having thousands of followers who forgot you existed a minute after following you.

You've probably been told that the more impressions a piece of content has, the more successful it is. This is wrong. Yes, 400,000 might have seen your YouTube video. But have they really seen it? Or did they click off it after two seconds?
Do they remember it? Did they interact with it? Are they now big fans of yours?
Can they name your brand?

Analytics never tell the full story. Yes, someone "saw" your video. But it doesn't tell you how much they interacted with it - or if they interacted with it at all. The amount of followers you have on Instagram only starts to matter when they care about you and what you're doing. Otherwise, they're totally irrelevant. They may as well not even be following you. Seriously.

A valuable audience on Instagram would be something like this:
You have 50,000 followers and 20,000 of them bought the book you advertised. That's an engaged audience, and that's what you need to aim for. Engaged followers are everything. They're your bread and butter.

Should You Buy Followers?
A lot of businesses get it into their heads that they should purchase followers. Hey, 100,000 purchased followers looks a lot better than 1,000 organic ones, right? Okay, it looks better. But what value is it adding to you and your business? None whatsoever. These purchased followers aren't going to buy from you. They don't even care about you. They're not your fans.

Look, a lot of the times numbers just don't matter. If you're going to spend your time showing off to people that you have 20,000 followers, good for you. But if only 1% of them are engaged with you and your content, nobody cares. Before you build a following, stop focusing on the numbers and start focusing on what value you're going to give to your audience.

Instagram has a good organic reach. If you have just 300 flowers, there is a good bet that around 140 will see your posts. If the posts are interesting and useful to them, they will consume your posts. In other words, they will engage and interact.

Twitter has a massive noise problem. Instagram doesn't. And you need to take advantage of that by shifting focus from number of followers to posting valuable content.

CHAPTER 4: HOW TO BUILD YOUR INSTAGRAM FOLLOWING

Now the hard work begins.

If you've ever browsed a friend's account on Instagram, you might have noticed that they have a LOT of followers, relatively speaking.

They're just ordinary people who do ordinary things, and who take ordinary pictures of seemingly ordinary things. Yet - despite having just 5 or 10 friends in real life - they have over 1,000 followers on Instagram.

"How did you get so many followers?" you ask them. "I don't know," they say with disinterest. They don't even care! If they can get that many followers without even trying, is it possible for you to get many more by trying? Totally!

Instagram is easily one of the best platforms on which to build an organic following on social media. It's much easier than both Facebook and Twitter. However, while it looks as simple as just posting pictures and watching followers flood through the gates, it isn't. Yes, amassing 1,000 followers can be as easy as that. But you don't want 1,000 followers. You want thousands and thousands.

The first thing you need to do is define your niche. What one thing are you offering? More to the point what is the one thing you are offering that's different - or at least better - than anyone else? What's your thing?

Secondly, you need to post a lot. Don't be lazy about this. Don't have a burst of excitement, where you post a flurry of pictures in two days, before losing interest and disappearing for a few weeks. People will forget about you.

Thirdly, when people like your photos, don't be egotistical about it. Respond by liking one of theirs! Show them some love, too. It's the same when someone comments on your photos. Comment on theirs, too. Interact. Be frigging social! Don't be a recluse who never leaves his or her own page. Venture out and network.

Fourthly, you need to use hash tags. People use hash tags for a reason. They don't use them as a gimmick. They use them so people who are searching for a particular something will find their posts.

These four things are prerequisites you absolutely need. Without them, you'll find it hard to build an organic following on Instagram.

As well as these four, there are other things you need:

Dedicate Yourself To Quality

If you dedicated yourself to quality and nothing else, would people come to you? Yes, very likely.

The comic strip artist and serial blogger, Scott Adams, described how he has "systems." What he means by this is that there are things he'll do consistently - such as blogging - without knowing where they will take him.

He used to blog a lot, but he wasn't making any money out of it. He was just doing it to see what would happen. He made a commitment to quality, so that whoever read his blogs would get value out of them. Eventually, his blog took off, secured him a publishing deal and made him lots of money.

He never knew it would come to this. But by consistently posting quality, people saw he was offering them value. They came to him, and it turned into a lucrative side business for Adams.

Quality always pays in the end. If you make a commitment to just one thing with your Instagram account, make a commitment to consistent quality. People will come to you because they love what you do. It adds value to their lives. They are genuinely interested.

Of course, the problem with this sort of commitment without knowing where it will get you is that it will take up a lot of your time. It will require a lot of effort on your part. And because it takes a good while to build a big following, there might be times when you feel like giving up.

However, once people see you're offering quality, they'll start to share your stuff. They will spread the word. This will lead to more followers over time.

Find Influencers And Engage With Them
If you've got a bit more time on your hands, and you don't mind being proactive, you should get your hands a bit dirty by finding influencers and engaging with them.

It's not too hard to find influencers in your field. All you need to do is search keywords and hash tags, and find the profiles that have lots of followers.

Then, you need to make a connection with them by liking and sharing their posts. Comment on their posts, and let them know you're here. After a bit of time, they'll take notice of you. They may follow you back, and even comment on your stuff.

Who knows? They might even share your stuff too, which will give you massive exposure to their audience.

Engaging with influencers and making it pay for you will take a bit of time. But it doesn't have to take a heap amount of time. In fact, it often serves as a quick way of building your audience.

Look at it like this: All it takes is one relevant influencer to share your post, and all of a sudden you could have hundreds - or even thousands - of new followers. It can be that easy.

It's recommended you don't just comment on one post and leave it at that. It looks too obvious you're just trying to draw attention to yourself. Instead, make an effort to ingratiate yourself in someone else's community. Take the time and effort to make a few good comments. Put yourself out there. Earn respect.

Give People An Incentive To Follow You

People on the Internet LOVE free stuff. Is there anything wrong with that? Not at all! You give them free stuff and in return they give us their following. It works out well for both parties. And in fact, most successful online entrepreneurs give MOST of their stuff away for free.

Holding contests, offering promotions, and giving cool stuff away for free is a fabulous way of getting more people to follow you. You could do something like, "Share this post with your friends and be in with a chance to win XXX." Or maybe you could do "Comment 'I'm In!' on this post to receive XXX." And you know what? People WILL like and share your stuff. People love good offers. If you can make an awesome offer, it will go viral.

However, there is a flipside: To make an awesome offer, you'll no doubt need to spend a bit of money in the first place. There will be an initial outlay. Moreover, you may attract lots of followers who are just there for the free stuff - they don't even know who you are or what you do!

Hey, it happens. But giving stuff away for free and regularly holding contests are an easy way of building up your Instagram following.

What About Bots?

You've probably heard that some people use Instagram Follow and Like bots to grow their audience. Why do they use these bots? Doesn't it mean they end up with a disengaged following?

Bots come in useful if you're finding it hard to build your following. They were designed to automate a few activities, such as commenting, liking and of course following. With their help, you can automate the process so that you save yourself some time.

Some of the most commonly used bots include Instagress and FollowLiker, although it seems as though each time a bot gets too popular, Instagram shuts it down.

Now, Instagram bots sound good in theory. Of course, anything that saves us time sounds good in theory. But like eating a whole cake to yourself sounds good in theory, bots can catch up with you afterwards, springing a nasty surprise. At first, bots tempt you with their time-saving skills.

"You've been so busy lately. Let me save you some time," they crow in your ear. But Instagram doesn't like automation. Of any kind. It's against their code of conduct, and it can get you banned. In short, it's best to stay away from bots if you intend to stay on Instagram for a long time.

CHAPTER 5: VARIOUS WAYS TO MAKE MONEY ON INSTAGRAM

The Internet is a great place because there are so many ways to make money. People like you have been making money on the Internet using YouTube, Facebook, their own personal blog and even from Instagram.

It's totally possible to make thousands of dollars per post on Instagram. It sounds too good to be true. But for once, it isn't.

At this point, you're probably thinking you need millions of followers to make significant money from Instagram. But the truth is that you don't. Not at all.

Exactly how many followers you need to make solid cash depends on a few factors. For example, the niche you're in plays a role, as does how engaged your followers happen to be. What's the point of having 100,000 followers when 60% of them are fake and 20% never interact with your posts? You could have just 10,000 followers, but as long as you explore the right revenue channels, you could make a bundle.

The key is building up engaged followers as opposed to just followers. There is a difference - a big difference. You could even have just 1,000 followers, but as long as 90% of them are fully engaged, the potential to make a profit is right there.

Here's a quick rundown of the ways you can make money from snapping and uploading pictures:

• Writing sponsored posts for brands that love your audience and want to get in front of it
• You could become an affiliate, which means you would make a commission each time you sell someone else's product
• Create and sell something!
• Offer a PAID service
• Sell your photography - this only works if you're good at taking pictures, and have a good camera

Also, remember that you don't have to chase just one revenue stream - you can chase multiples.

But first, let's dissect that first one a bit more - writing sponsored posts for brands who love your audience and want to get in front of it.

What this means is you've amassed an audience that sees you as an authority figure in a particular niche. They think you're awesome and trust what you have to say. Sweet! You're an influencer, a trendsetter, a go-getter. This is what a lot of brands want to be. But, for whatever reason, some brands just aren't this. In fact, they struggle to be this.

They want to be just like YOU but they don't know how to do it. The biggest thing they're envious of is the trust your audience has put in you. People trust you to give them sound advice, as well as sell (or give!) them products that are awesome and useful.

But despite enjoying high levels of trust, you might not be making the kind of money you want to make just yet. This where writing content for sponsored brands come in. Sponsored brands will pay you money in return for you writing something nice about them, and sharing their picture (or maybe you'd share a picture of yourself using their product.) You could even upload a video, if that's what the brand wants you to do.

Often, you'll post one thing and that's it. But sometimes a company will ask you to post an entire campaign, and sometimes they'll offer you freebies.

It's not easy to know what to charge these companies, especially if you've never done this before. But you need to remember that you're charging for two things:

1.) Great content
2.) Access to your awesome audience

Access to your audience is valuable alone. The best Instagram influencers charge up to $400 per post. Prices tend to start out from around $200.

But How Do You Find Brands?
Good question. A lot of the time, brands will find you - especially if you're big enough. But you should also do some sniffing around and seek out brands whose values and personality matches your own. That way, you won't get accused of selling out by your audience.

Don't be afraid of reaching out to them. Chances are, you're just the person they've been looking for this whole time, but didn't know where you were.

Becoming An Affiliate
You've probably heard about affiliate marketing, and how it's a great way to make cash on Instagram. Essentially, if you become an affiliate, you become a salesperson. You're no longer just trying to raise awareness for a brand; you're also trying to make sales for them. And each time you make a sale, you get a commission. If you don't make any sales, you don't make any money.

Becoming a successful affiliate on Instagram isn't easy because Instagram doesn't let you include links anywhere on your profile except your bio. This means just one link to a product at a time. Either that, or you can use a unique promo code for sales. Any links you use must be traceable, so that you get credit (and commission!) for the sale.

There are plenty of online merchants you could become an affiliate for. These include:

• ClickBank
• RewardStyle
• Amazon's Affiliate Program

Affiliate marketing is tricky, and it requires you to properly work out a plan. If you do that, you could make a decent amount of cash on the side.

Your Own Business
This eBook is for a personal user and business users alike. So, if you run your own business - such as an online store - Instagram can help you make more money.

What you're looking to do with Instagram is build your audience. Indeed, this is something all small online businesses struggle with. They might have a great product or service, but without an audience, they've got no one to sell to! Instagram can give you the audience you crave.

Naturally, an audience doesn't just appear. It's not the same as standing in a crowded city center, and whipping out a guitar to draw people to you. It's time consuming, and you need to be dedicated.

The good thing about selling your own stuff on Instagram (as opposed to someone else's) is you don't have to worry about their message, their brand and strategy. It's all yours - and all the money is yours, too. You can use Instagram to sell whatever it is you've got, from eBooks to online courses.

Selling Your Photos
Instagram is all about photos. But aside from uploading pretty pictures that attract likes and comments, you can also sell pictures. Photos can be assets on Instagram that you can license, print and ultimately sell.

If photography is what brought you to Instagram originally, you can use marketplaces like Twenty20 and 500px to list your photos. On here, you might find publishers and brands that are willing to license them. But you can also sell your photos directly to you

Instagram followers as prints or posters. It can be done - and you can make a lot of money doing it.

A great example is photographer Daniel Arnold, who could only afford toast for every single one of his meals each day. That is, until he made $15,000 in just one day on Instagram. He did it by selling his prints. He had:

A.) A demand for the prints
B.) An engaged audience

Take the bull by the horns. If you've got nice photos, don't wait for people to ask if they can buy them. Offer to sell them to anyone who wants them.

CHAPTER 6: CONTENT IDEAS THAT WORK

Ever had those Friday nights where you're excited to go out but realize you have nothing to wear? The excitement soon fades. How can you go out if you have nothing to wear? You sift through your wardrobe, flinging clothes onto your bed, as you get more frustrated, exclaiming, "I literally have nothing to wear." So, you call your friend and grumpily say you're staying in tonight.

This clothes analogy applies to coming up with content for Instagram. If you're fresh out of ideas, it's a nightmare. And even if you did come up with an idea for a new post, it's only one post. Tomorrow is another day and you'll be scratching your head again. If only you had content on tap.

This will be another problem you'll face: coming up with content that stands out from the crowd. That's really difficult.

However, there are things that work and don't work. There's actually a system you can use in order to churn out ideas. Here are some of them.

Show What Goes On Behind The Scenes

This is easy to do if you run a business, but it's not something people think of posting immediately. But guess what? Your audience wants to see what goes on behind the scenes at your business. They want a sneak peek

Show us the faces that make your business what it is. Show us your business is a community. Make a personal connection with your audience by giving them insight into what goes on at a small business.

With this kind of content, you don't need to be stuck for fresh ideas for a long, long time. There is always something you can show, such as:

• Your staff profiles
• A tour of your workplace
• Action shots of your staff busy at work
• Photos from staff nights out or events

Products
It seems like a no-brainer to post images of your products. But sometimes people are so caught up in posting pictures of food and daily adventures they totally forget to share pictures of what they sell.

This is important, too, because what you are selling is - in theory at least - what sets you apart from your rivals. As such, you need to make sure your audience sees it.

After all, isn't this what they're really interested in? Sure, a picture of your dinner looks appetizing. But what they want from you as a brand is a product that's going to solve a pain point.

Show them what you've got - but don't show too much of it. If all you post is your product, it's going to get boring and annoying pretty quickly. Promote your products, but not aggressively.

LifeStyle Is The Best Style
If you're in business, you should already know that good marketing is something that taps a particular emotion in the customer. Rather than just saying, "Hey, here is a pair of sunglasses that will protect you from the sun," you need to show how these sunglasses will make a person feel.

It's like car ads. How many times have you watched a car ad and thought, "What the heck does that have to do with a car?" It's because the brand is making you feel a certain way. They're saying that if you buy a Porsche, you'll feel like a million dollars.

This is something you can tap into on Instagram.

As you may have noticed, lots of entrepreneurs sell a lifestyle on Instagram. They're selling a product, but they're basically saying, "Buy my product and look at the great life you could be living, too!"

So they take pictures of themselves in expensive hotel suites, eating lobster, boarding private jets, working on said private jet, sipping champagne on sun kissed apartment balconies and so on. It's powerful stuff, because it makes you feel awesome. And pretty soon, you start associating feeling awesome with their brand and their product.

So think about who your audiences are. What are their interests? What are their aspirations? What would their dream life look like? Tap into this. Take photos that reflect all this. Show them you're already living their dream life, and that if they buy from you, they could live it, too.

Text And Quotes
Some Instagram profiles are basically just text and quotes - nothing else. Some people like it, others don't. However, it's perfectly okay to use texts and quotes once in awhile. It's an easy way of creating content when you're fresh out of ideas. You can even make it a part of your system.

People love inspirational, motivational, sweet quotes that make them feel good. Make sure your quotes and texts are relevant to your niche. If possible, use quotes from famous people.

For your text-based posts, you could post information about your brand. Keep the word count brief. Maybe you could use a text-based post to raise awareness of an event you're giving, or perhaps you could let us know some statistics related to your industry.

Repost User-Generated Content
You need to reach out to your audience, and show them you care about them. By reposting their ace content, you're showing them that you appreciate them. And if you're a big enough brand and they love what you do, you'll be making their day!

CHAPTER 7: MARKETING TIPS TO GROW YOUR BRAND

Instagram is a busy place, and it's currently home to over 500,000,000 users. That's a lot, even if it's considerably less than Facebook.

To reach even a fraction of those people, you don't need to be a marketing guru. You don't have to have taken marketing at degree level, or read all the books, or been to all the seminars. In fact, you can grow your brand on Instagram by implementing a few of the tips that are in this chapter.

These tips are all actionable, and they all work. Let's take a look.

Use The Free Instagram Tools
Did you know that Instagram now has business profiles, similar to the ones you'll find on Facebook? If you've got a business, it's time to take advantage of these profiles.

A business profile is much more useful to you than a regular profile. For one thing, you get a massive call-to-action that lets users text, email or even call your business.

You also get access to Instagram's analytics tool, which is known as Insights. This is invaluable. It lets you access engagement and impression data so you know how many people are seeing your posts, when they're seeing them, and how many are actively clicking your posts and interacting with them.

If you weren't aware of Instagram's business profile and still have a personal one, there is still time to make the switch. It's super easy to do, and totally worth it. Trust me. The more you understand your audience and their behavior, the more you can tailor content that they actually want to see.

Post Everywhere
Think the hard work is done when you upload a picture to Instagram? Nope. Not if you want to reach more people.

Cross promoting Instagram posts is what savvy marketers do. They know that there is a whole world beyond Instagram and there many more people who would like to see your posts. But until you start promoting them on other channels, such as Facebook and Twitter, they won't ever get to see them!

Not everyone on Instagram related to your field knows you exist. You can cast your net on Instagram, but you won't catch all the fish. So cast your net on Twitter, Facebook and LinkedIn, too.

Invite your army of Twitter followers to follow you on Instagram. Spread the word on Facebook. Don't be shy. Shamelessly self-promote yourself. It's what all the best marketers do.

Repurpose Other Peoples' Content
Is this one cheating? Not really. Just remember the famous quote by Picasso: "Good artists copy. Great artists steal."

Look, there will come a time when you're fresh out of ideas for what to post next. It's not always easy to come up with awesome new ideas for images, especially if you're not a visual person.

It's okay to be stuck now and then. If you are stuck, it's recommended that you take a look at other profiles related to your niche and see what they're doing. What kind of content are they putting out there that you could rehash for your own audience?

It's important that you don't brazenly steal someone else's image. Be inspired by what other people are doing, but make sure you put your own personal stamp on it so that you can't get into trouble. If you must steal, credit the other profile by tagging them.

Ask For Your Followers' Email Address
Email isn't Instagram. But Instagram is just another link on the chain to getting your followers to take the action you want them to take.

Think of your Instagram followers as leverage or leads. The more followers you amass, the more people you can sell to. And selling gets a lot easier once you have someone's email address. So why not ask them for their email address?

Once you get customers to opt-into receiving email newsletters from you, you're in a strong position to make more sales and grow your business. Email marketing is relevant in 2017 - very relevant. If you can shift your Instagram followers to email, you're a winner. But how to do this?

Naturally, you can't just ask someone for his or her email address. You need to give them a reason to opt-into your email newsletter. You can do this via a call to action. Simply post an image, and tell your users to sign up to your email newsletter if they want to receive awesome content and free stuff from you on a regular basis.

Once you have their email address, you could even start interacting with them on a one-to-one basis.

Don't Forget Videos

Thought Instagram was all about images? Think again. Video marketing is huge. People love videos and when they see short, snappy videos on Instagram, it makes them happy. In fact, it makes them happy enough to follow your page and comment.

Videos get people talking. So post them. A warning though: Your videos must be good. Sounds obvious, right? But it's so easy to make a mess of videos.

Use Sponsored Ads

Lastly, and perhaps the best marketing tip of all, you should consider using sponsored ads if your budget allows.

Sponsored ads help you target your audience in a new, better way. They're especially awesome if you're just starting out on Instagram, have few followers, but know you've got an awesome image that people would love if they saw it. They also put your images in front of people in your demographic that aren't already following you.

CHAPTER 8: HOW TO USE INSTAGRAM ANALYTICS

Okay, so you can see how many people have Liked your posts, and you can see who's commented. But this sort of information is useless. It tells you nothing about your audience and their behavior, and it's not going to help you grow your profile.

Key to understanding your audience, including who they are and what they want to see from you, is Instagram Analytics.

Understanding your Analytics can be daunting. After all, you need to work out things like data and metrics. It can be confusing. But first of all ...

Do Analytics Really Matter?
Yes, it matters. Understanding your Analytics isn't as simple as knowing which photos and videos are your top performers. It's all about an in-depth understanding of how your audience relates to your content, as well as changing trends. The knowledge you will gain by studying your Analytics will be invaluable.

Analytics is especially good at showing you how well two posts perform against one another in a straight shoot-out. Let's say you run an eCommerce store, and want to know how well one product photo performs against the other. One photo is set against a dark background, while another is set against a light background. You can use engagement data to find out which of the two consistently performs better than the other.

You can then go and see how well your products shots compare versus your behind-the-scenes content. If it turns out that your audience prefers behind-the-scene stuff, it might be time to double down on that while spending less time on product shots.

Without this knowledge, you may end up repeating mistakes - ergo, wasting time with content your audience isn't interested in.

Analytics is Artificial Intelligence. And although this might be hard for you to admit, the truth is that AI knows your audience better than you do.

Using Instagram Analytics To Understand Your Audience
It all starts with knowing demographics. In other words:

• How old your audience is
• Where they live

• When your audience most frequently interacts with your content

Let's start with your audience's age and gender.

Once you know how old your audience is on average, you can then start posting suitable content. Memes, for examples, won't go down as well on people aged fifty and over as they would on a much younger audience. You would also avoid using frequent pop culture references.

The next thing you should consider is your audience's location. While this won't necessarily affect the type of content you post, understanding the average location of your audience should determine when you post. For example, let's say you operate in Europe and post your content at a time that would suit European audiences.

But what if your core demographic lives in Asia or America? Take a look at the top cities, and then adapt your schedule to suit them.

Engagement, Reach And Impressions … What Does It All Mean?
Engagement, Reach and Impressions are all metrics. But what kind of metrics are they?

Impressions refer to the total number of times your post was viewed. Total views include repeat views. For example, just because a post was seen 500 times, it doesn't mean 500 different people saw it. Many people could have viewed it twice or even three times.

Reach narrows things down a bit, and refers to unique views. This is handy, as it cuts out all those repeat views that can skew your metrics.

Engagements, meanwhile, refers to each time someone engaged with your content, either by liking, commenting or saving. It doesn't count numerous comments from the same person - which is a good thing, because that sort of thing can distort your data.

Engagement Rate refers to the percentage of people who have engaged with your posts.

Follower Growth
Follower Growth is handy, as it lets you know exactly how many new followers you have acquired in the past week.

When you first start out on Instagram, Follower Growth isn't necessary. You can easily see how many new followers you have. But as the weeks go by, you won't have the time to keep checking to see how many new followers you have.

Follower Growth also includes all the followers you've lost as part of its calculation, and it gives you a good indication in regards to how fast your profile is growing.

Let's Break The Metrics Down Between Stories, Videos And Photos

Metrics are usually calculated the same, whether you're looking to gather data about your stories, videos or images. However, this doesn't mean you should be comparing videos versus images versus stories.

Why? Because the user experience is different from one type of content to the next.

Images versus Videos [i]

Yes, both videos and images appear in someone's feed. But the way people interact with one or the other is very different. And this has a big impact on performance.

For example, images are easy to spot and like. You can literally take one second to make up your mind whether or not you're going to like it or comment on it.

With videos it's a bit different. Some videos are slow to load, and some are long. As such, if you're in a rush, you might decide against hanging around until it loads. The result is no like or comment. As you can imagine, videos acquire less engagement than photos.

Since you can't count on likes and comments to help you understand video performance, you need to turn to views.

And a view is officially registered after three seconds. This doesn't matter whether you've got a 30 second long video, or a 3 second GIF. It's the same.

Instagram Stories
A photo doesn't require active engagement from users. Neither does a video, relatively speaking at least. But Instagram Stories do.

To engage with the content, a user needs to tap your story at the top of your feed. They can then either watch your story in full, swipe out or tap through. As such, you can find out your Stories' replies and exits, as well as their reach and impressions.

What are Exits?

Exits refer to the amount of times a user has left your Story before it's finished. This doesn't always mean they had a bad user experience and didn't enjoy it. It means, for example, that they decided to click a hyperlink placed by you just before the Story finished. Maybe they got a bit giddy and wanted to take things forward ASAP.

However, more often than not, Exits is a useful metric that lets you know how successful your Stories are, and therefore what you need to change about them to make them even more successful.

What are Replies?

Replies are similar to engagements for your videos and images. But unlike public comment on your videos and images, replies to a Story always end up in your inbox.

Choosing Which KPI's To Use For Your Instagram Strategy

Now that you know the different metrics that Instagram offers to help you understand more about your audience, it's time to work out what our KPIs are - in other words, your Key Performance Indicators.

A KPI will be your preferred metric which measures specifically how successful (or unsuccessful) your campaign or content is. You will choose which KPIs you use based on what you're looking to get out of Instagram, as well as what your business goals are.

For example, if your business needs community to be successful, engagement will be your main KPI. Basically, if community makes or breaks your business, you need engagement.

But if you decide to boost a specific post, you will then need to change your KPI, and instead focus on your reach. Why? So that you can see what a bigger portion of Instagram's community thinks of your post.

Another KPI could be comments. For example, let's say you decide to hold a contest. You ask your followers to reply with "I'm in!" if they want to participate in the contest. You then use this metric (comments) to determine how successful your contest campaigns are. How many people are commenting? How many aren't? What's wrong with the contest?

Improving Your Content Strategy With Instagram Analytics

Now that you know a fair amount about metrics and KPIs, you can start to tweak your content so it's the kind of content your audience really wants to see.

You might be tempted at the moment to focus on an individual post that got a whopping 2,000 likes, and declare your profile is a success but one hit wonders are not what you should be looking for.

Instead, you should be looking for patterns. If you don't look for patterns, but instead decide to have a celebration whenever 1 post out of 30 suddenly gets ten times your usual amount of engagement, you're doing it wrong and your content won't improve.

Moreover, you have to remember why 1 post out of 30 suddenly gets way more engagement than usual. Often, it is purely luck. Perhaps more people are on holiday, or perhaps it's just a busy news day.

Having said all that, data is not the be-all and end-all. It's not a magic bullet. If you focus too much on it, you will limit your creativity.

Don't be a slave to data. Being a slave to data can make your content creation worse, as you start imposing strict rules upon yourself. You still need some wiggle room, and you need to keep your creative hat on. Just listen to your intuition. Play around. Have some fun. If you find something that really sticks, ride the wave. Double down on it.

CHAPTER 9: DEADLY MISTAKES TO AVOID ON INSTAGRAM

Instagram is a great way to establish a strong Internet presence and make some cash. Get things wrong, though, and it could turn out to be a total disaster.

If you don't know what you are doing and enter Instagram without focus or a clear plan, there are easy mistakes to make that could cost you big time. To save you the hassle, this final chapter will highlight the deadly mistakes you need to avoid.

Creating Instead Of Documenting

There are a lot of people who have a hard time creating fresh content for their Instagram profile. And when they do have an idea, they spend a lot of time executing it.

There was this Instagram account that would post definitions of unusual words. The girl whose Instagram account it was told me that it used to take her ages just to make one post. She'd have to find a relevant image for each word, add the definition, make sure the font size was right and so on. It took her like an hour to make just one Instagram post. A whole hour. Why? Because she was creating and not documenting.

When you create, you lose time. You lose time thinking of a neat new idea, and you lose time executing it. When you document, you save time.

What does documenting mean? It means simply documenting your day. When you do something related to your niche that your followers would appreciate, take a picture and upload it. It's that simple. You're documenting your day. You're not creating. And you're saving a heap of time.

Using The Wrong Hash Tags
You've heard all about hash tags, and you're aware that people use them to catch peoples' eyes.

Indeed, hash tags are a massive reason why total strangers find your posts in the first place. Without them, you'd be hidden. While you may be tempted to try to hijack the most popular hash tags, it never works.

Why? Because you simply can't hijack a popular hash tag. You don't have enough followers or enough of a presence to dominate a hash tag that everyone else is using.

It's like when small businesses uses a popular keyword and expect people to find them on Google. No one will find them because the most popular keyword is being used by far bigger companies than theirs. In other words, the competition is too strong.

It's a much better idea to forget all about popular hash tags and focus on ones that are relevant and more specific to your niche. It might take some time, but eventually people will find you.

Using Too Many Hash Tags
Another easy mistake you can make when it comes to hash tags is using too many. You might have seen some profiles that use lots and lots of hash tags. Maybe it's okay for your friends to use plenty of hash tags. But if you're a business owner using Instagram, you need to be a bit more professional.

Too many hash tags looks unprofessional, and it can clutter up your posts. Use relevant, targeted hash tags, but don't overdo it. You want all the attention to be on your images, and not on your tags.

Spamming
When you first open an Instagram account, it's tempting to post a lot. People all get a bit giddy to start with. You may have so many ideas, and end up posting

way too much. People got annoyed with this and some might even unfollow you.

Yes, you want to post stuff and raise awareness of your brand. But too much posting only harms your brand.

It's a good idea to schedule your posts so that you don't overdo things. IconSquare is a good tool that helps to this end. It shows you your posting analytics, and lets you know when the best times to post are.

Making Your Account Private
Okay, so making your personal profile private is entirely up to you. But if you want to amass lots of followers, it's a massive No No.

Some businesses still make their accounts private. It makes zero sense. When your account is private, it means followers have to request to follow you. And then they have to wait until you get round to approving their request. This can sometimes take days; depending on how slow a user is in reacting to the request.

Worse still, until you've approved their request, they can't see your content. And think about it. If they can't see your content beforehand, why would they even be motivated to go ahead and follow you? What have you got for them?

Recycling The Same Old Content

The problem some people have is that they're not the best at coming up with fresh content. This is especially troublesome if they operate in a small niche.

Let's say you're a writer trying to sell your stories. After posting quotes and book covers, where do you go next? There are actually plenty of different types of photos you could post. But too many users don't take the time to think outside the box, and they end up recycling the same old stuff. But the same old thing quickly gets boring. It gets old.

CONCLUSION

To sum up, Instagram is a great place to go and grow your brand. Your audience is on there. They're waiting for you.

The last advice that you should take heed is simply to show up. By this, it means post everyday if possible. Be there every other day if you can't make it every day. Post fresh content often. Follow people. Interact, Like and Comment.

Don't let your account fall by the wayside. Keep on top of it and watch your engagement and followers grow.

THANKS FOR READING

We really hope you enjoyed this book. If you found this material helpful feel free to share it with friends. You can also help others find it by leaving a review where you purchased the book. Your feedback will help us continue to write books you love.

The Smart Reads library is growing by the day! Make sure and check out the other wonderful books in our catalog. We would love to hear which books are your favorite.

Visit:
www.smartreads.co/freebooks
to receive Smart Reads books for FREE

Check us out on Instagram:
www.instagram.com/smart_readers
@smart_readers

Don't forget your 2 FREE audiobooks.
Use this link www.audibletrial.com/Travis to claim
your 2 FREE Books.

SMART READS ORIGINS

Smart Reads was born out of the desire to find the best information fast without having to wade through the sheer volume of fluff available online. Smart Reads combs through massive amounts of knowledge compiles the best into quick to read books on a variety of subjects.

We consider ourselves Smart Readers, not dummies. We know reading is smart. We're self taught. We like to learn a TON about a WIDE variety of topics. We have developed a love for books and we find intelligence attractive.

We found that each new topic we tried to learn about started with the challenge of finding the pieces of the puzzle that mattered most. It becomes a treasure hunt rather than an education.

Smart Reads wants to find the best of the best information for you. To condense it into a package that you can consume in an hour or less. So you can read more books about more topics in less time.

OUR MISSION

Smart Reads aims to accelerate the availability of useful information and will publish a high quality book on every major topic on amazon.

Smart Reads hopes to remove barriers to sharing by taking the copyright off everything we publish and donating it to the public domain. We hope other publishers and authors will follow our example.

Our goal is to donate $1,000,000 or more by 2020 to build over 2,000 schools by giving 5% of our net profit to Pencils of Promise.

We want to restore forests around the globe by planting a tree for every 10 physical books we sell and hope to plant over 100,000 trees by 2020.

Doesn't it feel good knowing that by educating yourself you are helping the world be a better place? We think so too...

Thanks for helping us help the world. You Smart Reader you...

Travis and the Smart Reads Team

WHY I STARTED SMART READS

Every time I wanted to learn about something new I'd have to buy 20 books on the topic and spend way too long sorting through them and reading them all until I arrived at the big picture. Until I had enough perspectives to know who was just guessing, who was uninformed and who had stumbled upon something remarkable.

I wished someone else could just go in and figure that out for me and tell me what matters. That's how smart reads was born. I want smart reads to be a company that does all that research up front. Sorts through all the content that is available on each topic and pulls out the most up to date complete understanding, then have people smarter than me package the best wisdom in an easy to understand way in the least amount of words possible.

For example, I got a new puppy so I wanted to learn about dog training. I bought 14 different books about dog training and by the time I got through the first 5 and finally started getting the big picture on the best way to train my puppy she had grown up into a dog.

Yeah she's well behaved. She doesn't poop in the house. I can get her to sit and come when I call. But what if someone else went in and read all those books for me, found the underlying themes and picked out the best information that would give me the big picture and get me right to the point. And I'd only have to read one book instead of 15.

That would be amazing. I would save time. And maybe my dog would be rolling over, cleaning up after my kids and doing the dishes by now. That my friend, is the reason I started smart reads. Because I wanted a company I can trust to deliver me the best information in an easy to understand way that I can digest in under an hour. Because dog training is one of many subjects I want to master.

The quicker I can learn a wide variety of topics the sooner that information can begin playing a role in shaping my future. And none of us knows how long that future will be. So why not do everything we can to make the best of it and consume a ton of knowledge. And I figured all the better if I can also make a positive difference in the world.

That's why we're also building schools, planting trees and challenging ideas about copyright's place in today's world. Because as a company we have to be doing everything we can to support the ecosystem that gives us all these beautiful places to read our books. Thanks for reading.

Travis

Customers Who Bought This
Customers Who Bought This Book Also Bought

Twitter Marketing Strategies: Smart Tips on How to Monetize Your Followers

How to Master Email Marketing: Your 1-Page Marketing Plan to Grow a Massive Email List, Make Money and Build Your Brand with Email

Writing on the Internet: Learn SEO Tips & Techniques and Become a Successful Online Writer

Email Marketing 101: How to Gain Subscribers, Grow Your List and Make Sales

How to Market and Sell Your Online Course in Udemy: Tips and Tricks on Making Money Teaching an Online Course

The Everything Store Sales Guide: How to Make Money with Amazon FBA

Passive Income: Do What You Want When You Want and Make Money While You Sleep

Understanding Affiliate Marketing: An Internet Marketing Guide for How To Make Money Online Using Products, Websites and Services